How Shall We Celebrate?

Embracing Jesus in Every Season

How Shall We Celebrate?

Embracing Jesus in Every Season

Lorraine V. Murray

With illustrations by Jef Murray

Resurrection Press
An Imprint of
CATHOLIC BOOK PUBLISHING CORP.
Totowa • NJ

First published in March, 2005 by

Catholic Book Publishing/Resurrection Press
77 West End Road
Totowa, NJ 07512

ISBN 1-878718-97-5

Library of Congress Catalog Card Number: 2004117494

Cover design and inside illustrations by Jef Murray

Printed in the United States of America

1 2 3 4 5 6 7 8 9

To my sister, Rosemary, and cousins, Julie and John, for sharing childhood joys and woes with me; to my Aunt Rita and Uncle Ray, for their gift of enduring love; and to my husband, Jef, for providing a happy home where stability, affection—and good food—abound.

And in memory of my beloved parents, Grace and Gaspar Viscardi, who surely are celebrating today in heaven!

CONTENTS

"The Holy Ghost over the bent world broods with warm breast and with ah! bright wings."

–Gerard Manley Hopkins
"God's Grandeur"

ACKNOWLEDGMENTS

I AM grateful for the people in my life who understand a writer's somewhat eccentric ways, especially this writer's need for encouragement and feedback, and generous stretches of solitude. My husband, Jef, is first on the list.

Saturdays are special days for us. After breakfast, he heads to his studio with a pot of tea, and I settle in front of the computer with a mug of coffee. We both spend hours trying to spin a few lovely webs—me with words, him with oil paints. By early afternoon, we are done; he washes the paint from his brushes and I turn off the computer.

Then we don our straw hats and go for a long walk, huffing and puffing up the hills of Chelsea Heights, and often discussing any snarls that may be threatening my latest newspaper columns. Writing the book you hold in your hands was a special joy because it was a shared endeavor with Jef, who has decorated the stories with his pen-and-ink drawings.

My spiritual father, Monsignor Richard Lopez, has given me the great gift of his wisdom, friendship and prayers, and I am eternally grateful to him.

How thankful I am to the children who inspire me without knowing it. The little ones who so often lift up my heart are my goddaughter, Sarah Mottram, and her brother, Stephen. My great niece and nephews, although far away, still have a special place in my heart: Brok, Monet, and Bradenton Mende; Lakely and Austin Smith, and the latest member of the family, Noah Metcalf.

My mother-in-law, Lou Craig, encourages Jef and me by celebrating the passages in our lives, whether they are birthdays, art shows or books. It is a great delight to hear her voice on the phone, telling me she enjoyed one of my columns. I'm also thankful for the love showered on me by my sister, Rosemary

Mende; my sister-in-law, Lisa Murray; my Aunt Rita and Uncle Ray; my best friend, Pam Mottram; my nieces, Christina and Jenifer; my nephew, Rick; and my cousins: Julie and Charles Anderson; Debbie and John Rosasco; Father Christopher Viscardi, S.J.; and Anthony and Eleanor Vertullo.

I am blessed with faithful friends who show an interest in my writing: David Ivie, Rose Dilday, Susan Liebeskind, Jeff Donnell, Claire Evans, Bob and Fran Wiggins, and Jack and Edna Friel.

For many prayers and kindnesses, I thank Father John Azar, pastor of St. John Chrysostom Melkite Greek Catholic Church, and the congregation, who have welcomed my husband and me so graciously into their midst.

I'm also grateful to editors who publish my work regularly and give me helpful feedback: Kevin Austin, the editor of the Faith and Values section of *The Atlanta Journal-Constitution,* and Mary Anne Castranio, executive editor of *The Georgia Bulletin.*

Others who have been supportive of my writing are my colleagues at the Pitts Theology Library, especially M. Pat Graham (and Doris), Marianna Anderson, Eran Tomer, and Fesseha Nega.

Over the years, I have been blessed with e-mails and letters from so many kind and supportive readers of my newspaper columns. They have prayed for me, encouraged me, shared their stories with me—and helped me see that, even though writers work in solitude, their words can connect them with a very large communion of saints!

Emilie Cerar at Resurrection Press is a special angel in my life. A wonderful editor, she shaped the publication of my first book, *Grace Notes,* and has shepherded the book you are now reading. Thank you, Emilie! I will always cherish your editorial insights and your friendship.

FOREWORD

T HE religious and secular feasts and memorials of the year
reflect our need to call to mind and heart significant experiences. Be these experiences personal, universal, religious, or
secular, they have in common our need to set aside a day that
rises above the ordinary. On these days, we are helped to
remember, to share some common experience, in large part
through the labor of others. Indeed, our feasts and memorial
days are days of remembering. And because we remember,
we can also hope that we learn good things through our years,
good things to give, to share, to cherish. Remembering is not
only about the past. It has much to teach us about our days
and years ahead.

In this wonderful book, Lorraine V. Murray has gathered
reflections on thirty commemorative times of the year. She
remembers days and seasons and writes of them as she has
taken them to heart over the years. Each entry is a delight-
fully crafted invitation to share in her loves, her hopes, her
disappointments, her faith, her honesty. The entries are ac-
companied by delightful pen and ink drawings, which were
done by Jef, Lorraine's husband. As I read *How Shall We
Celebrate?* I found myself over and over again remembering
experiences from my own recollections of secular and religious feasts days and better understanding them in light of
Lorraine's tender approach to the important times on our
calendars.

How Shall We Celebrate? has as its subtitle "Embracing
Jesus in Every Season." Our years pass swiftly and all of us
have a treasure trove of memories that can rise to the surface

on any given season or celebratory day. Yet as near as that treasure is–for it is within us–we need a gifted other to help us find it and take from it. A writer whose gift is the craft of words can be just what we need to find the gold that is in our hearts, our memories. What I love about this book is how Lorraine takes very ordinary things and weaves them into the rich fabric of special days. It is "where" the ordinary events of our lives best fit. She takes what has been given to her and offers it back to the reader in holiday garb–lovely, inviting, redemptive and, I might add, eternal.

It is Jesus who knocks at our hearts every day of our lives. In our busyness–or, perhaps, a looking and listening for him in places other than our lived experience, we miss him. *How Shall We Celebrate?* is a book that places that gentle knocking on the door of our own hearts. Page after page are further revelations into the extraordinary power of the seemingly fleeting and mundane, revelations that allow holiness to be seen in and through the ordinary.

Lorraine writes of what she calls "chipmunk moments." These are moments when an experience of joy or wonder, delight or peace, enters one's life as suddenly and surprisingly as a chipmunk. The little creatures are as elusive as they are delightful. But they do scamper across our paths. This reminds Lorraine of the unplanned for entry of the divine into our lives. She calls "chipmunk moments" the "ordinary events that remind me of the Creator's love." This little book is filled with such moments. I picture Lorraine, writing in solitude, remembering such moments and writing of them–sharing them. It is a beautiful gift and she shares it beautifully.

–*James Stephen Behrens*
Monastery of the Holy Spirit

INTRODUCTION

I'VE long been enamored of devices marking the passage of time. I started keeping a diary when I was seven years old, and some days all I had to record was "Nothing happened." Still, I wrote in the green leather-bound book faithfully, locking it with a tiny gold key each night.

My first encounter with religious calendars came during Advent, when my mom displayed, in a prominent spot in the living room, a festive cardboard house with diminutive windows etched on it. Each day during the four weeks of Advent, I thrilled to open a window where little angels or stars peeked out as reminders that Christmas was drawing nearer.

These days, like so many folks, I rely on various calendars to pull together the bits and pieces of my life. There is the religious calendar we pick up at church on Christmas, which shows the liturgical seasons, like Advent and Lent, plus saints' and feast days. I also rely on an ordinary calendar to keep track of secular events like Labor Day, Father's Day and Thanksgiving.

At the start of each year, I sit down with my new calendars to circle the important dates, so I can send birthday and anniversary cards to the people I love. One day, as I was marking the dates, a thought occurred to me: Why not have a calendar that would weave together secular and sacred days of the year? From that thought, this book was born. It is a celebration of 30 special days of the year, some taken from the liturgical calendar, and some from ordinary life.

The notion of including Labor Day and the spring equinox in a book that also celebrates Passion Sunday and Mary Magdalene's feast day might seem a bit of a stretch, but the spirit of Jesus breathes in the heart of every event, whether it is worldly or sacred. For example, although we often bemoan the commercialization of Christmas, Jesus remains at the heart of the traditions. After all, Santa stands for "saint" and reminds us of St. Nicholas, a holy Christian man who loved the poor; the evergreen tree signifies eternal life–and the abundance of lights symbolizes the birth of the one who was called "the light of the world."

Even days typically considered non-religious invite us to feel God's presence in our lives. For example, Midsummer Night's Eve, the longest day of the year, is rarely noted on religious calendars, but the glorious lingering of the sun is another reminder to Christians that Christ can vanquish the darkness of sin.

During medieval times, there was no separation of the sacred from everyday life. Church bells rang each day at noon so that everyone could stop what they were doing and say a short prayer. Farmers dropped to their knees in the fields and women followed suit in the kitchen, all praying the Angelus, a simple prayer that commemorates the Incarnation.

"The angel of the Lord declared unto Mary, and she conceived of the Holy Spirit," were the words that united everyone, from the simplest peasant to the most powerful ruler. Today, the prayer has nearly vanished from the traditions of lay people, but members of many religious orders still pray the Angelus at noon.

My prayer is that this book will take you on a splendid journey throughout the year, from the promise of Advent traditions to the sparkle of Christmas; from the sparseness of Lent to the exuberance of Easter; from summer's lush gardens to winter's still landscapes. May you celebrate and cherish

God's presence in every ritual, from the lighting of Advent candles to the planting of a summer garden.

The closer you dwell on the worldly and the supernatural, the more you discover there is very little difference. As Gerard Manley Hopkins so nicely put it: "The world is charged with the grandeur of God." That goes for every calendar day as well.

Advent

O, Dayspring

IN days of old, when I was a youth, Christmas decorations never showed up before Thanksgiving. This year, alas, downtown Decatur was decked out in lights the day after Halloween, and Santa held court at the mall shortly thereafter.

In our haste to celebrate Christmas, we often forget about Advent, a four-week stretch that signifies the opening of a new liturgical year and takes us to Christmas Eve. Advent means "coming" and marks a time of spiritual preparation for the Christ child's arrival, while also reminding Christians that we are awaiting the Second Coming of Christ.

Waiting is not very popular in our world today. We rush through express lanes at the grocery store and hasten home to prepare microwave suppers in minutes. Mornings find us downing fast-food breakfasts and zooming to the office to dash off a few quick e-mail replies. Some things, though, can't be sped up, thank God. The sun moves to an ancient timetable beyond the reach of human hands; it still takes nine months to grow a human baby, and a whole hour to bake a loaf of decent pumpkin bread.

When we rush too much, time melts like chocolate on a blistering summer day. If you've ever experienced an over-scheduled weekend, where you ran from shops to soccer games to parties, then you may recall that Monday found you feeling like you'd never had a weekend at all. The reason is simple enough: The more activities we cram into the precious moments of our lives, the faster time goes—and the more frantic we feel. If you want to slow down time, try sitting in a chair for ten minutes without a book, TV show or any other diversion. You will be astonished at how the hands of the clock seem to creep along when you stop filling every second.

Advent invites us to put the brakes on our harried lives. So often, Christmas is here and gone before we know it, and we are sitting in front of our mound of new stuff, draining the last drop of eggnog from the cup and feeling weary. Advent traditions let us savor the moments leading up to the big day. Each year, my husband and I put together a simple evergreen wreath and secure within it four candles, one pink and three purple. The pink symbolizes joy and the purple a turning of our hearts toward God.

Each night of Advent, we gather to read scripture and pray. Traditionally you light one candle the first week, then two candles during week two, and so on. You replace all the candles with white ones, representing Christ, on Christmas day. We also place an empty crèche in the living room, with a handful of straw nearby. When family members do charitable acts, which ideally remain anonymous, they add a piece of straw to the manger. The goal is to create a comfortable place for the baby by Christmas day.

Advent beckons us to hope. It reminds us that, no matter how awful our world may seem at times, with diseases, wars, and so many other miseries, God never abandons us. Or as the 14th century mystic Julian of Norwich put it: *"All shall be well."*

When the baby who changed the course of human history was born, there was no room for him at the inn. Advent gives us a chance to take a deep spiritual breath as we wait for that baby. A chance to promise ourselves that, no matter how busy we may be, we will always make room for our beloved Jesus in our hearts.

St. Nicholas—December 6

Goodness Sake

THAT'S me in the black-and-white photo, the chubby girl with a horrified look on her face. The big guy upon whose lap I am perched is none other than a department store Santa—and no wonder I look scared. The man was larger and furrier than the men in my family, and hadn't I been warned about talking to strangers?

Fortunately, as the years passed, I conquered my fear of conversing with the man who represented jolly old Saint Nicholas, although it wasn't long before another dilemma developed: I began confusing him with God.

After all, the two share much in common from a child's perspective. Santa has a list of the good kids and the bad ones, and is reputed to know when you're sleeping and when you're awake. God is supposed to be omniscient, which means He keeps an eye on us at all times. Santa miraculously travels all over the world on Christmas Eve, transported by reindeer that defy the laws of gravity. He resides in a mysterious place called the North Pole, where he hangs around with wondrous creatures called elves. Methinks this sounds a bit like heaven and angels.

Like most children, I believed that if I were good, the god-like Santa figure would deliver my heart's desires on Christmas, whether they were fancy outfits for my dolls, some plush stuffed animals—or perhaps a nice pair of baby gerbils. However, there were many years when I was as virtuous as gold and still didn't get everything on my list. Although I didn't know it at the time, now I realize that my parents couldn't afford to make all my dreams come true. A friend who grew up poor recalls his mom telling him that Santa had limited resources, which meant that if one child got everything he wanted, other kids would get nothing. Maybe it's an important lesson for children to realize that, even if you're good, you don't always get what you want.

Children who think virtuous behavior gets rewarded may grow into adults who jump on board the prosperity gospel bandwagon, which claims that God answers the prayers of the faithful by showering them with wealth. Surely you'd have to wear blinders to believe in that kind of God. All over the globe, decent people are suffering from the effects of poverty, famine, disease and war.

The Book of Job probably contains the keenest insights into the vexing question of why the prayers of apparently good people sometimes go unanswered. Job was a decent and pious man, a sterling husband and father. One day, out of the blue, all hell broke loose, so to speak. His children died; he was stricken with a terrible illness; and he lost all his worldly goods. Long story short: Job ranted and raved, but never gave up his faith because he recognized that if we accept blessings from the hand of God, we must also accept troubles. In the end, he stopped envisioning God as a benevolent Santa figure and drew closer to the mystery of God in the process.

Believing in a Santa Claus version of God, who rewards nice kids with their hearts' desires, can lead to huge disappointments. After all, Joseph and Mary didn't get that room at the inn on the night of Jesus' birth, but they did just fine anyway. Besides, whether we're naughty or nice, we are still God's children. And although He may fail to give us everything on our wish list, He never stops doling out the one gift we really need, which is His merciful love.

Christmas—December 25

Angels Vigil

WE are lined up outside a church on the Emory University campus on an achingly cold night. Inside, the congregation has gathered to hear The Nine Lessons and Carols, performed by campus groups since 1935.

About 200 of us stand shivering in identical black robes, holding unlit candles and awaiting our cue to enter the church. We have been rehearsing faithfully for the past three months under the expert eye of Director Eric Nelson, who has drilled us on every nuance of singing. Earlier tonight, during our warm-up in the empty church, Eric reminded us why we are here. This concert is not just a performance, he said, but rather our gift to the people who gather here on this dark night, seeking hope.

Now a young woman walks through the crowd, lighting a few singers' candles. We carefully share our flames with the others while I whisper a nervous prayer: "Please, God, don't let me sing off-key or trip. And please don't let me set fire to the church." At the doorway, a feisty gust of wind threatens to quench our candles, but we manage to get into the church, fire intact. We find our way toward the stage, singing about a baby born among the meek and lowly, while the congregation sits in expectant silence.

Tonight, Scripture and songs tell ancient stories of light banishing darkness and joy triumphing over gloom. We sing about a baby as radiant as the morning star, a child who conquered the dark shadows of death. "O come, O come, Emmanuel," we chant, inviting him into our hearts.

The stories tell about angels revealing impossible things in dreams. A virgin would give birth; God would humble

Himself to become human. They tell about Mary and Joseph, simple people who embraced the unthinkable by saying, "So be it." One reading describes Jesus as the light that came into the world; it reminds me of how we keep our faith alive by tapping into the fire in other people's hearts. Some days, I trudge to church, feeling dull and uninspired, and then I am stunned by the look on a young mother's face as she kneels in prayer, or by the sound of a toddler proclaiming "alleluia" as best he can. And in that moment, my soul is rekindled.

My heart is racing with anticipation now because we are leaving the stage. This is the moment when darkness again descends as we circle the congregation, intoning our last song: "Sleep, sleep . . . the angels vigil keep, while Mary takes him to her breast and bids him close his eyes and rest."

In the velvety darkness, I shiver as I sense what is happening. Christmas, I realize, is not merely an historical event that happened long ago, and we are not just singing a carol to an audience. In some mysterious way, we are crooning a lullaby to the baby who was born in that simple stable long ago—and who is springing to life again in our hearts at this moment.

Now, as I see one candle lit, and then watch as the flame passes from singer to singer until a chain of light connects us, I remember what tonight is really about. It is about hope. About a wondrous spectacle that can't be seen through the lens of logic, but only with the eyes of love. Then, as the last note drifts into the stillness, we turn and walk slowly out, still cradling our tiny flames. No one says a word. After all, we don't want to awaken the baby.

Holy Innocents
December 28

Lambs of God

I'VE just read about a husband and wife who yearn desperately to have a baby. Problem is, the man has a severe deformity and they're afraid the baby might inherit the gene that caused it.

Prenatal genetic testing seems the obvious solution. If the gene shows up in the fetus, the couple would have the option of terminating the pregnancy and trying again. Still, a deeper look reveals something horribly wrong with this picture. In short, it is one thing to sort through a batch of peaches and discard the imperfect ones, but when we are talking about human beings, it is quite another story.

A biblical passage assures us that not one sparrow falls to the ground without the Father's knowledge. How much more carefully, then, must God keep watch over new human lives, whether they carry "bad" genes or not. Truth be told, there is a more personal reason why prenatal testing makes me shudder. You see, it is possible I carry the gene for breast cancer, which means that, had my parents had access to this testing, they might have decided to terminate the pregnancy and try again.

Now I realize that proponents of prenatal testing believe that eliminating flawed humans means less suffering for people in the long run. Still, if you ask the less fortunate people–like me–I suspect they would say they are ecstatic they had a chance to be born.

Today, the fetuses in danger of being discarded have genes linked to Down Syndrome, heart defects, cleft palates and dwarfism. Deafness, blindness, cerebral palsy and some forms of cancer are also on the defect list, which grows longer each day.

The world is brimming with "defective" people, but many go on to make enormous contributions to mankind. The writer Flannery O'Connor was stricken in her twenties with Lupus, a genetically transmitted, incurable disease, but she continued writing fiction that today is celebrated as some of the South's finest writing. A wondrous example of the truth that physical imperfections don't mar the soul, O'Connor wrote, "You will have found Christ when you are concerned with other people's sufferings and not your own."

Obviously, not every person afflicted with a genetic disease will turn out like Flannery O'Connor. Still, every person has a place, however humble, in God's plan.

The book *Waiting with Gabriel* recounts Amy Kuebelbeck's heart-wrenching journey after doctors told her when she was five-and-a-half months pregnant, that her baby had a heart defect and would die within days of being born. She and her husband never considered ending the pregnancy, but instead found support from family and friends who helped them bear the burden of the unthinkable: preparing for a birth and a death simultaneously.

Gabriel lived only two-and-a-half hours and died peacefully, but in his humble time on earth, he changed the world forever. His life and death prompted the birth of his mom's book, which I trust will comfort countless other parents walking the same tragic path.

Jesus reminded us to invite the poor, the lame and the blind to our banquets, but sadly they are the ones that today might end up in the genetic reject pile. He also assured us that God sees the sparrow fall. But wouldn't it sound more impressive to say God sees the hawk or the eagle? They are, after all, far more spectacular birds.

Still, I believe Jesus chose the humble sparrow for a reason. To remind us that God's love is unconditional. It embraces not just powerful, impressive people, but all of us. No matter how weak, flawed—or downright defective—we may be.

New Year's Day

Poor Banished Children

I AM at a New Year's Day clearance sale, where the garments are screaming, "Buy me," and I'm trembling with desire for that tantalizing sweater, those glittering earrings, and, oh, those svelte shoes.

Suddenly, I'm drowning in a sea of neediness. I've forgotten that I live in a roomy house and own a decent car and, let's face it, have more clothing than I could possibly wear out in a lifetime. I'm like Eve wandering around the Garden of Eden. Instead of rejoicing over those thickets of trees, a loving mate, and the chance to chat with God, Eve was obsessing over what she didn't have: that famous forbidden fruit.

Wish I could have had a word with Eve. "Girlfriend, look at your life!" I'd say. "Are you going to take a chance and blow the whole thing just because you think that tree over there is better than the rest?" But I fear Eve would turn a deaf ear. After all, when I'm on an envy roll, there's no stopping me. No wonder, when Satan traipsed by, she was putty in his hands.

As I wander through the store, I realize we are all daughters and sons of Eve, and, like her, we chase after forbidden fruit, which today comes in many shapes and colors. "If only," we sing to ourselves, "if only I had a bigger car, a better job, the trophy spouse, a beach house ... then at last I'd be happy."

The media provide us chilling models of folks who have the whole fruit basket but are still miserable. Movie stars make millions a year and can buy all the goodies they crave. Too often, though, they struggle with infidelity, broken families, drug abuse and alcoholism. Not a pretty picture.

Please don't get me wrong: I am not saying we should walk around wrapped in humble cloaks and eating plain porridge.

Obviously, things like rocking chairs and cozy sweaters can bring us great joy. Still, I am aware that many items that I consider necessities, like air-conditioning and a car, are luscious luxuries in the eyes of most of the world.

Truth to tell, I'm spoiled rotten. I have never gone to bed hungry, unless you count those stupid diets in college, and the only time I suffered from the cold was when we lost power during that nasty ice storm a few years ago. And, yes, I complained bitterly.

Still, yearnings spring up endlessly in my soul. A pretty dress demands matching earrings; a new purse begs for trendy shoes. One desire births a thousand more. I often feel like I'm peering through a window at a candy store, where folks are gorging themselves on sweets, while I'm chewing on rice cakes.

In my younger years, I believed that *if only* I bagged a graduate degree, I would be perfectly content. Got that. Then I longed for marriage. Got that. Then I yearned for a house with all the trimmings. Chalk that one up too. Still, happiness is so elusive, like a dazzling butterfly swooping across a meadow as I trail behind with a broken net.

"My soul is restless, O Lord, until it rests in Thee," wrote St. Augustine long ago, and his wisdom echoes in my heart today. The truth is that material goods and achievements will never satisfy us. But maybe, with prayer and God's grace, we will one day stop chanting, "If only." And on that day we will realize that our deepest longings can be fulfilled only by God and we will change our tune to a simple "Thank you."

Valentine's Day—February 14

All Loves Excelling

I REMEMBER my first clumsy efforts at cutting hearts from red paper to create a valentine for the person I loved most in the world, my mom. No matter how crooked the edges were, she always praised my cards as if they were priceless pieces of artwork. She exclaimed over the fine way I printed my name, and then posted my creations on the refrigerator door. And although my mom died over 25 years ago, each Valentine's Day I recall the lessons about love she taught me.

She told me it was all right to be different, and I really needed to hear those words because I didn't fit in anywhere. I was a fat, awkward little girl, always last chosen for teams. While other girls had boyfriends who slipped them valentines, my mailbox was conspicuously empty.

In high school, when all my friends were agog about the senior prom and I didn't have a date, I remember standing on the front steps with my mom, a big Miami moon smiling down at us, as I confessed my heartbreak. And I remember the way she took me in her arms and assured me that sweethearts would come in time.

She taught me you stick by the people you love, no matter what. My dad had a gambling problem and so money had a way of slipping through his fingers. In the days before gambling was recognized as an addiction, my mom had to get a job to keep the family financial ship afloat, but she never pointed a finger of blame at my dad.

I learned from her that people you love sometimes are so vexing that you have to take dramatic measures. When my sister and I were particularly rambunctious, my mom would pack a small suitcase and then drive around the block in the family car. We always knew she would come back, but the gesture shook us back into obedience.

She also taught me that love transcends time. I remember walking into the kitchen when I was a teenager and seeing her weeping over a batch of cookies she was making from her mother's recipe. When she told me the tears were for her mom, I was at first baffled. Her mom had died when I was a baby, and it took me a while to understand that the bond between mother and child is eternal, and whether a child is 10 or 50, memories of mom always tug at the heart.

More than anything, though, my mom taught me about compassion. When she was in the final stages of cancer, I went with my dad to see her at the hospital. She noticed I was coughing and sneezing, brushed her lips against my forehead, and then worried aloud that I was running a fever. I wanted to stay with her in the hospital, but she insisted I go home and get a good night's sleep. For the rest of my life I will remember that on the night she died, my mother was fretting over my well-being.

I still miss my mom, especially on Valentine's Day, but I believe she's in heaven, a blissful place where she can peek into my life now and then, and nudge me gently in the right direction. And this Valentine's Day, I will give my mom the most precious thing I have, the same gift I gave her as a child. I will give her my heart.

Mardi Gras / Fat Tuesday

Behind the Mask

SOMETIMES, when I'm watching a film, I experience what I call the "chills-up-and-down my-spine" reaction, which is a rare event. For example, although I enjoyed the Harry Potter movies, there were no big revelations—and definitely no chills.

Spider-Man 2 is a different story. Although I am not a huge fan of action films, the Spidey tales are impossible to resist, and it's because good and evil are so clearly delineated. Black is black, and white is white, and morality is non-negotiable.

The dreams of the awkward, young Peter Parker are easy to identify with. What he wants are the same things we all want: a home, a job, a decent car—and someone to love. He yearns to be just an ordinary guy, who can get to places on time rather than being swept into some big adventure along the way.

"Am I not supposed to have what I need?" he complains to his aunt.

But God apparently has other plans for Peter Parker, who possesses gifts like superhuman strength and agility. And in *Spider-Man 2,* we see him struggling to navigate the unusual path God has given him.

His eminently sensible aunt sets him straight. What counts in life, she says, is doing what is right, which sometimes means sacrificing your own dreams. Her down-home advice echoes the biblical admonition: "Whoever seeks to keep his life will lose it, and whoever loses his life will preserve it."

What a shocking message, though, for audiences who have cut their teeth on the "I did it my way" school of life. We have been told we deserve everything, and that includes good looks, big bucks, elegant houses and snazzy cars. We should "Just do it."

If we're aging, we call the Botox doctor. If our physique is less than perfect, we buy implants or take little blue pills (depending on our gender). If our spouse doesn't thrill us, we take a lover. Fortunately, there are extraordinary people in our midst who swim against this tide, and who will instantly understand the aunt's message.

They are the unsung heroes of the world. The men and women who dreamt of college but instead are working two jobs to support their families. The parents pacing the floor at night with squalling infants. And the weary couples that looked forward to a sleek retirement but instead are raising their children's children.

Peter Parker's turning point comes when he sees that his longing to be an ordinary fellow will literally cost people their lives. His decision to don his Spider-Man costume once again turns him into a true hero–a word, by the way, whose roots suggest serving and protecting others. And the chills-running-up-and-down-my-spine scene happens when Spider-Man stops an out-of-control train filled with frightened passengers –and then passes out from the effort.

The passengers realize he has risked his life to save them. And as they ever so gently lift the unconscious young man above their heads, passing him from person to person, their expressions radiate awe and love. Although he is a total stranger, for just a moment he is their beloved child.

And the chills come big time when I realize that Spider-Man reminds me so much of another hero. He was a man who lived long ago in Nazareth. He was both servant and protector, and was willing to give up everything–even his life–to do what was right.

Lent

Fast Times

I AM a major sugar addict. When I am blue, nothing works better than chocolate to lift my fallen spirits. If I'm celebrating, I dig into a dish of ice cream, and if I'm anxious, I head to the cookie jar.

And here we are in the middle of Lent, a time when millions of Christians are following Jesus into the desert, where he fasted and prayed for 40 days. I thought long and hard about my fast this year, studied my cornucopia of addictions, and saw that I had, alas, many choices. I could fast from recreational shopping, drinking wine, worrying or complaining. However, these would be easy compared to what I finally chose, which was, sigh, sweets.

Embracing self-denial can seem downright masochistic in a world where we are taught to buy the latest gizmos and gadgets in an endless quest to be comfortable. Still, although the word "fasting" brings to mind ashen-faced saints huddling in sparse cells and wearing itchy hair shirts, it does have its benefits. After all, whether you choose to eliminate TV, sweets, red meat or gossiping, you stand to gain some insights into your personality. But be forewarned: They are not necessarily pretty.

As for me, I am becoming vividly aware of how petty I am. It's sad but true: Christ spent 40 days among wild animals in the desert, enduring thirst and hunger, and yet I feel like a big martyr because I had to pass on the cupcakes yesterday. And don't get me started about peanut M & M's. To me there is no music lovelier than the crinkly sound the bag makes when you open it with your teeth, and the delicate clatter of chocolates pouring into your hand.

When Jesus went into the desert the devil showed up, which is no big surprise, since the Prince of Darkness never misses a good opportunity. The devil tempted a famished man by encouraging him to turn stones into bread, and Jesus refused. Evidently the devil knew that if a hungry man spotted a loaf of bread, chances were good he'd break his fast. And Satan delights in broken promises.

Since childhood, I've broken countless promises to myself after embarking on diets to lose a few pounds. I have pilfered numerous calories while maintaining a saintly countenance among my friends. "I can't understand why the diet isn't working," I have whimpered, not mentioning the bag of cookies hidden beneath my bed.

Truth be told, in previous Lents, I have approached fasting like a guilty dieter and failed miserably. This year, though, I reminded myself that fasting is a gift to the one who suffered hunger for 40 days and nights. By holding that thought, I am hoping to make it to Easter morning without a single peanut M.

But of course, wouldn't you know it: Satan has pitched a tent in my desert—and keeps reminding me about the cake stashed in the freezer. Devil's Food, of course. Still, despite his temptations, the good news is this: It has now been 508 hours since chocolate has passed my lips, which I assure you wouldn't be happening without sweet helpings of God's grace.

On Easter morning, I hope to announce that I have evicted Satan from my Lenten desert. I yearn to be among the millions of Christians celebrating the glorious wonder of Jesus rising from the dead. Along with another, smaller miracle. It's called keeping our promises.

Spring Equinox—March 20

Earthly Cares

WHAT joy! After a long winter, the world is coming to life again! Daffodils are poking their buttery heads skyward, while pear trees do their best imitation of clouds. The squirrel that resides in our birdhouse emerged recently to sun himself upon its roof, and outside our window a persistent Carolina wren, no bigger than your thumb, trumpets a melody loud enough to wake the dead.

Welcome to spring, a time when chicks peck their way out of shells, and rabbits rouse sleepily from hollows to mate and produce miniature versions of themselves. Nature echoes the mystery of rebirth lying at the heart of faith: Bare wintry limbs, which seemed dead, now heed a secret signal to send forth tendrils of green.

How do trees know what to do—and do it so predictably? Even the most ardent atheist has to shrug his shoulders and admit ignorance of this ancient, perfectly attuned dance of nature. "The world is charged with the grandeur of God," wrote my favorite poet Gerard Manley Hopkins. "It will flame out, like shining from shook foil." And I can only say, "Amen."

"Where is God?" was one of the earliest catechism questions I learned. Although I didn't appreciate it then, the answer was rather poetic: "God is everywhere." Too often, we envision God perched on a throne in the clouds, while planet Earth spins along, a place where humans sweat and labor until one day we join Him in the Great Beyond. We lose ourselves in our world of cell phones, laptops and television, while outside in our yard, God is producing a five-star show. Especially in spring, we can see God's imprint everywhere. Really, in a zillion years, could any of us have designed anything as elegant and lovely as the weeping cherry tree? As triumphant as a star magnolia in full bloom? Or as impossible as a butterfly emerging from a cocoon?

Some religious holidays seem so ensnared in earthly things that folks bemoan the apparent lack of the sacred. For example, as Easter approaches, the grocery store shelves are laden with stuffed rabbits, baskets of green grass and marshmallow eggs. We might think such trappings miss the whole point, until we realize it makes sense to celebrate resurrection at a time when nature itself is doing just that. After all, everything about this time of year heralds new life: the humble egg, newborn animals and even a lady's Sunday hat bedecked in flowers.

After the Resurrection, Christ appeared to his disciples on the road to Emmaus and walked a long way beside them. They didn't recognize him, though, until he broke bread with them. What an ordinary moment. No trumpets. No choirs of heavenly hosts. Just plain old bread. Surely if we can encounter divinity in something as humble as bread, then we can find God in the grandeurs of spring.

You must be attentive, though. Keep a close watch on the arms of trees sprouting fine green fuzz and applaud the cheery faces of hyacinths. Keep an eye peeled for elusive chipmunks, warming their whiskers in the sun. Don't forget that spring also beckons us to celebrate our own rebirth after bleak wintry days. We made it through flu season and did not succumb to the latest round of scary viruses. Whatever was broken, whether it was heart, knee or spirit, is on the mend.

Now the heart exults in rabbits, chicks, sprouting greenery and the serenade of wrens. We break bread with friends, walk down the road with them—and come face to face with God.

Palm Sunday/Passion Sunday

Jesu Dulcis

THERE has been a surprising stirring of media interest lately in someone whose name rarely makes headlines: Jesus Christ. And although other movies have portrayed his life and death, Mel Gibson's *The Passion of the Christ* is sparking intense controversy and debate. Too bad some critics seem so intent on deciding who bears responsibility for the crucifixion that they've turned the story into a major whodunit. The truth is, though, that Christ's death is not a mystery to be unraveled, but a love story to be embraced.

How fitting that Jesus performs his first miracle at a wedding feast. When his mother tells him the couple has run out of wine, his compassion sparks the transformation of water into wine. Another chapter in the love story unfolds the night before he died, when he stooped down to wash the disciples' feet. And he didn't just bathe the feet of the faithful; he included Judas, the one who would betray him for 30 pieces of silver.

The danger of taking Christ's final hours out of context is that he can appear to be merely a revolutionary figure, arrested and crucified against his will for bucking the status quo. But Christians believe Jesus was much more: We believe he was God in the flesh. And his suffering on the cross is the jewel of our faith, through which shines our hope of life after death.

Jesus' passion and death were part of God's plan to redeem mankind ever since Adam and Eve fell from grace. Jesus knew the whole plan and told his friends exactly what would happen: "The Son of Man will be handed over to the chief priests and the scribes, and they will condemn him to death; then they will hand him over to the Gentiles; they will mock him, and spit upon him, and flog him, and kill him; and after three days he will rise again" (Mark 10:33-34).

As a child, I didn't understand why Jesus had to suffer. Couldn't he have died peacefully as an old man surrounded by his friends? And if he knew he was going to be crucified, why didn't he run away? Later, I realized Jesus himself answered these questions by saying, "No one has greater love than this, to lay down one's life for one's friends" (John 15:13). He willingly endured a horrendous death out of love for all mankind, past, present and future. He came into the world to redeem the war-torn, the weary, the sick and the hungry. Looking in the mirror, I am stunned to realize he died for me.

The awe and mystery of the passion story is that God, pierced and bloodied, endured suffering and death to tell us the one thing we have such trouble believing: He loves us.

And when we find ourselves in our own private Gardens of Gethsemane, only Jesus' passion can make sense of our suffering. Because the cross shows us God isn't removed from our agonies. Instead, He weeps with us.

My favorite Gospel story comes at the end of John's narrative. Peter and the disciples are fishing when they spot a man on the shore. When they realize who it is, Peter jumps overboard and swims toward him, while the rest follow in the boat. The man is the Risen Jesus and he is cooking fish over a charcoal fire. What joy the disciples must have felt to realize he was still taking care of them. And what a perfect closing scene in a love story that goes on forever.

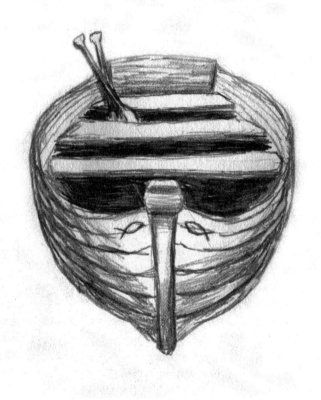

Holy Thursday

Ubi Caritas

THIS is make-it-or-break-it week for Christians. Friday marks the crucifixion, followed by the celebration of the Resurrection on Sunday. Either you embrace the miracle of Jesus suffering an agonizing death, and then emerging from the tomb three days later, or you don't. And during this auspicious and sacred week, I am a little embarrassed to admit what I have been pondering. In a word, feet.

We have so many expressions about feet. We talk about folks having one foot in the grave, and others being footloose and fancy-free. There is also putting your best foot forward, putting your foot down, and inserting your foot in your mouth. And if you want to be insulting, just ask someone to kiss your foot.

In the Gospels, people were always throwing themselves at Jesus' feet and sitting at his feet. Two women anointed his feet, one with tears and one with precious oils. Maybe it was not so outlandish that, on the night before he died, he was thinking about something as humble and down-to-earth as feet.

I can just see the scene. He rises from the supper table, ties a towel around his waist, pours water into a basin—and bends down and starts washing his friends' feet. Peter protests vehemently. After all, bathing someone's feet is the work of a servant, and Peter is in awe of his teacher.

To make matters worse for poor Peter, feet really took a beating in his day. Folks walked long distances in sandals over dusty roads—and baths were few and far between. Still, Peter finally gets the point: He surrenders his tootsies to Jesus, grime and soot and all.

In that moment, I wonder if he felt like a little child again, lovingly tended to by his mother. Washing someone, after all, is such a basic act of love. My earliest memories are of my mom soaping me up in the bathroom sink, inventing funny songs while I silently adored her with my eyes. Years later, when my nephew, Rick, was born, my mother, sister and I followed that tradition, scrubbing the pink little fellow in the sink and singing to him. I remember holding one of his plump feet in my hands–and, yes, kissing it. I wondered where his feet would take him, once he was all grown up.

Christ's feet took him on a long, harsh journey. They took him up the mountain to pray, and into the desert to fast. Those same feet scared the living daylights out of his friends that stormy night when they saw him walking on water. His feet also traipsed into the lonely Garden of Gethsemane the night he was arrested where he wept because he sensed what was coming. How weary those feet must have been on the day when he was condemned to death and had to carry that heavy cross to the hill. How broken they must have been when he was pinned brutally to the cross.

Beneath his cross was Mother Mary, the one who had bathed him as a child and who surely, now and again, had planted a kiss on the feet she saw impaled on the cross above her. Her faith sustained her as she stood there. She knew it was not the end for her beloved son, but the beginning. And for Christians, what sustains us through this holy week is the same assurance. We trust that the one whose hands and feet were nailed to the cross emerged from the grave triumphant and still walks with us today.

Good Friday

Grace in the Cross

"I WISH none of this had happened." I was watching *The Lord of the Rings* with my husband, when these words, spoken by a hobbit named Frodo, sent chills down my spine. They were the same words I had uttered, so many times, after my breast cancer diagnosis five years ago. And they reminded me of the millions of people crushed by suffering, whether from illness, war, poverty or the agonies of old age.

Tolkien, the author of *The Lord of the Rings,* was a devout Catholic, and his work shimmers with Christian imagery, says author Bradley J. Birzer in *J.R.R. Tolkien's Sanctifying Myth.* The author suggests that Frodo's endurance of the suffering that comes with the ring mirrors Jesus' acceptance of the agony of the cross.

The cross stands for the terrible things in our lives that we'd like to wish away. The cross can be a marriage crumbling, a child dying or a disease striking. It can be a terrorist attack, an earthquake or a car wreck. "Why did this happen?" we weep, and maybe we shake our fists at God.

If we are fortunate, perhaps we are blessed with a friend like Gandalf, who offers sage advice. "I wish none of this had happened," Frodo says, with tears in his eyes. "So do all who live to see such times, but that is not for them to decide," Gandalf replies. "All you have to decide is what to do with the time that is given to you." And then he adds: "You were meant to have (the ring)."

His words express the fiercest challenge of our faith: accepting that horrible things can happen to the nicest people. Faith means smiling through your tears at the doctor's office. It means crawling out of bed on the morning after your mother's funeral and somehow getting through the day.

After my cancer diagnosis, I did my share of weeping and moaning. For a long time, I was utterly obsessed with the cross I was hauling around, which seemed bigger than anyone else's. And then one day, I looked around and saw evidence of the cross everywhere. I saw it mirrored in the eyes of a young mother paralyzed after a car accident and imprinted on the aching back of an elderly friend. I saw the cross in the tears of a woman whose husband had jilted her. And finally, I saw the truth: No one, no matter how beautiful, rich or powerful, escapes suffering.

Can the cross be a gift? Somehow, that suggestion seems almost unspeakable in a world where we do everything we can to avoid suffering. Still, acceptance of the cross may work mysterious changes in our souls. Frodo, for example, loses his innocent, happy-go-lucky attitude, but grows a bigger heart. As for me, I doubt that I would have written three books without my particular cross. I didn't give my self wholeheartedly to my writing until I recognized that I wasn't going to live forever.

Do I wish the cancer had never happened? I am no saint, so I admit that on most days that is my wish. But I also realize the cross has transformed me forever. The endless compassion of family and friends has revealed the hand of God in every corner of my life. And I'm learning, little by little, that whenever we surrender to God's plan, there is one gift we can always expect. It is the grace to endure whatever crosses may come.

Easter

Trinity

IT IS Easter morning, and eggs, hard-boiled, dipped gaily in dyes and tucked away in secret baskets, are awaiting the eager grasp of small hands. Although they seem so commonplace, eggs are rather mysterious in their own simple way. Our pagan ancestors evidently thought it a most startling event to see a new living creature emerge from a seemingly dead object, which may explain how eggs came to represent the transforming power of faith.

And on this special day, when the humble egg plays such a prominent role, I find myself reflecting on three women who have shown me how faith can transform our hearts.

The first was Jesus' mother, Mary, a simple peasant girl who said, "Let it be" when an angel came to deliver the stunning news that she would bear a child. There is a powerful testimony from Mary in Luke's Gospel called "The Magnificat," which shows her joy over her spiritual transformation. "My soul magnifies the Lord," she says, "For He has looked with favor on the lowliness of His servant. Surely, from now on all generations will call me blessed."

The second was Mary Magdalene, a woman from whom Jesus expelled seven devils.

Having one demon surely is more than enough, but seven? We can imagine she was quite a wreck to start with. And after she has been healed, she becomes a follower of Jesus, and later, in some Gospel accounts, is first to arrive at the empty tomb. When Jesus' other friends get scared and leave, she stays behind, crying, and sees a man she believes is a gardener. It's only when she hears his voice that she recognizes Christ, which is a perfect moment, given that he earlier said that sheep always recognize the shepherd's voice.

As an aside, I don't buy any of that *Da Vinci Code* nonsense that Mary Magdalene was Jesus' lover. That makes for intriguing fiction, and that's what the book is, but the problem is that some folks have taken the work as factual. How sad that in a sex-drenched society we have to paint even Jesus with the brush stroke of lust. What is so beautiful about this particular twosome is that they were platonic friends to the end, and beyond.

If you want an historically accurate titillating tale, try the story about St. Mary of Egypt, who lived in the fourth century. After many years as a prostitute, she one day joined a pilgrimage to Jerusalem, not for saintly reasons but because she was on the prowl for potential clients.

One day, Mary tried to walk into the Church of the Holy Sepulchre, but found herself flung backwards by some unseen being. Frightened, she prayed before an icon of the Blessed Virgin and repented of her dark sins. On her next try, Mary entered the church effortlessly and then fell to her knees to venerate the Holy Cross. She later fled to the desert and lived as a hermit for over 40 years.

The promises of Easter are manifold: Those who say "yes" to God shall become blessed, those who are tormented by demons shall be healed, and those who fall by the wayside shall be forgiven.

Out of the emptiness of the tomb, new life emerges. The angel proclaims the good news: "He has risen, as he promised." And as Christians dig into our baskets of eggs on Easter morning, we taste the mystery of the Resurrection. Like the three Marys, we believe faith can transform us. And we trust that we too shall be reborn from the broken shells of our past lives.

First Holy Communion

Living Bread

I WALK into the kitchen, rummage through the cupboards and then line up the ingredients needed to produce a miracle: flour, water, yeast and salt. It is bread-making day.

Baking bread always calls me to the mystery of transformation. The flour came from wheat, given life by sun and rain; the yeast has been sitting in the refrigerator, waiting to be revived with warm water and a pinch of sugar. When I first started making bread a few years ago, the whole process seemed like a mysterious ritual that I'd surely get wrong. Fortunately, the dough survived my clumsy massaging and did what it was supposed to do: It rose.

Today, as I knead the dough, I think about the first Saturday in May, when a beloved little boy named Stephen, our best friends' son, will consume consecrated bread and wine on his First Holy Communion day. As Stephen has been taught in school, long ago Jesus ate a humble meal with his friends and left them a simple, but astonishing, admonition. They were to consume bread but eat something else–his body. They were to drink his blood in the wine.

I remember my First Holy Communion so well. The photo on my dresser shows a chubby girl decked out in a frilly white dress and veil, standing beside her beaming mother, adorned in a fine dark suit with matching pumps. I recall the sweet clusters of flowers on the altar, the flash of rosary beads in children's hands and the fragile whisper of the girls' crinolines as we processed up the aisle. When it was my turn, I approached the altar, my hands clasped carefully–just like Sister had taught us–and knelt before the priest. As he placed the moon-shaped sliver of bread in my mouth, I felt I was about to meet Jesus in a special way. Back in my pew, I bent my head and poured out my heart. Holy Communion beckoned me to communicate with God.

The simple acts of eating and drinking embrace so many miracles. From a mother's breast comes milk that gives life to the baby. From grapes come wine. From Christ's hands comes the Communion banquet that nourishes us on a deep, mystical level.

As a child, I learned that God had humbled himself to become human. Later, I realized that Communion mirrors the Incarnation. The humble substances of bread and wine are exalted to become God.

Growing up, I loved the line in the Lord's Prayer: "Give us this day, our daily bread," which is a perfect prayer for children, who so sweetly trust that their everyday needs will be met. These days, I often yearn for more than daily sustenance. "Please, God," I pray, "let me keep my family and friends, my health, my faith. Don't let anything change."

Now the kneading is done, and as I put the dough in a warm spot to rise, I reflect on God's grace, which works like yeast in my soul, slowly changing me. Sometimes I get impatient, though. Why am I still so selfish, so bitter and so unforgiving? How long do I have to wait for God to heal my heart? But bread also calls me to patience; I can't rush the rising of the dough.

Hours later, when the bread is done and its aroma is perfuming the house, I take the first bite and thank God as I realize that the miraculous transformation has happened again, as promised. And this is my prayer for Stephen and all children making their First Holy Communion: May the miracle also happen in their hearts.

Mother's Day
Second Sunday in May

Eyes of Mercy

WE are walking into the narthex of Sacred Heart Church, when suddenly our little goddaughter, Sarah, spots a plaque on the wall that sparks her interest.

"Aunt Lorraine, who is that?" she asks.

There are so many answers to this question, but the child is barely 6, and I want to keep things simple. So I tell her the picture shows Mother Teresa, who was a very holy woman. I also mention that Mother Teresa attended Mass in this very church in 1995–and can't help adding, "Your uncle and I met her when she came to Atlanta."

I am drawn back in time to the day we attended the consecration of the Gift of Grace, a home for indigent women with AIDS, where a Mass was to be celebrated with Mother Teresa in attendance. We were huddled, elbow to elbow with many other volunteers, waiting for Mother to show up, when suddenly the back door opened and in trailed a line of diminutive nuns, dressed in identical white saris edged in dark blue.

One nun was particularly bent over, and when a woman near me reached out to touch the hem of this lady's robe, the nun turned and I looked directly into her eyes–and surprised myself by bursting into tears.

There was something about the open, childlike expression that shook me to the core. Later, another volunteer summed it up perfectly by saying, "You see Christ in her eyes."

My attention returns to the present as little Sarah asks solemnly, "Is she dead?" When I answer yes, her mouth quivers and then she dashes outside to play with her brother. I can't tell Sarah today, but some day when she's older I will explain about the special connection that exists between her and Mother Teresa.

While Sarah was still in the womb, her mother, Pam, faced a surgery that could not be postponed. When I shared this worrisome news with Mother Teresa's nuns at the Gift of Grace, they began praying for the twosome and gave me a medal blessed by Mother Teresa to give to Pam.

My friend's surgery went splendidly; the baby was born perfectly healthy. Shortly after, Pam asked my husband and me to become Sarah's godparents, which was a huge gift to us. Each Mother's Day, this little girl hands me a box of something yummy, sometimes chocolates, and other times homemade cookies, plus a special crayoned card, which often shows a big stick figure or heart ("That's you") and a smaller one ("That's me"). Invariably, as I exclaim over the treats, she chimes in with the question I love so dearly: "Can I have one?"

On the anniversary of her baptismal date each year, we celebrate the moment we became linked as spiritual mother and child. Sometimes I throw her a teddy bear tea party, and other times we bake cookies and play with stuffed animals.

There is so much to tell this little girl about the relationship between us, but here's the most important thing: It is eternal. No matter what happens, even if we are separated geographically, she will be my beloved spiritual daughter, and I will always pray for her.

And when she is older, I will tell her something that has touched me time and again, ever since the first moment I glimpsed her face. Whenever I look at this lovely girl, I see in her eyes that look of wonder and innocence that I saw long ago in another pair of eyes at the Gift of Grace Home.

The Visitation—May 31

Rosa Mystica

THE roses are alive! I am thinking as I head out into our garden, trailed by a persistent orange wasp. Invariably, after pruning my roses in February, I fear I have killed them and will never see another bloom. And then in May comes my big glorious surprise: Out of apparent death emerges the most luxuriant beauty.

A little research reveals that the rose was the flower of Aphrodite, the Greek goddess of love and beauty. In Roman times, it became the flower of Venus as well. Early Christians shunned roses because they linked them with paganism, but by the Middle Ages, roses, especially white ones, came to symbolize the purity of the Virgin Mary, while thorns were linked with Christ's bloody passion.

As a child, I loved the feast days of Mary when my classmates and I brought in roses and other flowers from home and placed the blossoms at the feet of the statue of Mary. Some of the flowers we wove into a simple crown for her to wear. It was a child's way of saying, "I love you."

How fitting that rosary beads, so closely connected with Mary, were originally made from dried roses. Ever since I was old enough to pray, I have been praying the rosary or, as some would say, "telling the beads." As a child I took these prayers very seriously. I knew that praying the rosary would help the souls of the faithful departed gain entry into heaven.

And so I dutifully prayed for my favorite uncle, the handsome Johnny Rosasco, who had died tragically young, leaving behind my Aunt Rita and two babies, Julie and John. I also prayed for my grandparents on both sides, whom I had never met. And because children don't make much distinction between humans and animals, I even stormed heaven for my departed turtles. The worn holy card tucked away in my prayer book said it all: "Pray for Wormy and Flat-top."

Today, as I pray the rosary, I recall that, according to legend, when Mary makes an appearance among mortals, they often perceive the powerful aroma of roses. I also remember that, on the day my mom died, my sister's house was mysteriously filled with this very scent, although no flowers were present. A mystery, we all said at the time. And later I wondered if Mother Mary was visiting us to announce: "All is well. Your mom is with Jesus and me in heaven."

Dear Mary's life reveals grace in surrender. Her humble acquiescence to become the mother of God changed the world forever. She was a woman who survived a mother's worst nightmare, watching her beloved child die an agonizing death. And surely some of the saddest words in the Gospels are the cry of Jesus while dying: "I thirst" and the description of Mary, who "stood there at the foot of the cross." After the crucifixion, her faith never wavered. She was in the room praying with the apostles on the day when the Risen Christ appeared among them—and oh, how I wish someone had described the expression on her face!

Each May, when my roses turn their lovely faces to bask in the light of the sun, I think about Mother Mary. About how she and dear Joseph were the first to behold the visage of the one called the "light of the world." Mother Mary encourages us to keep our faces toward the sun, no matter how bad things may get. And in times of trouble, when we thirst for mercy and love, she assures us that, after even the harshest pruning, there will come new life.

Ordinary Time

Kyrie Eleison

"HOW'S it going?" I ask a college student passing my desk. "Same old, same old," she replies, then pauses. "But maybe that's a good thing."

What joy to detect wisdom in one so young, I think, and reflect that, in my own youth, I scorned routines. Instead, I was a major adventure hound. You name the trend and I jumped on board. Sneaking out of the dorm and partying all night? Did that. Getting chased by the National Guard during a peace demonstration? Did that. Experimenting with drugs—and inhaling? I was there.

I grew up in a strict Catholic household, and I couldn't wait to leave home for college, where I shrugged off the dictates of my faith like a snake sheds its skin. I shudder to admit it, but my favorite hobby was shoplifting small items of clothing in department stores. When my conscience yelped, I assured myself that the stores were stealing from me anyway, and I was just settling the score.

I vowed I would not lead a boring life. When my classmates graduated and went on to marriage and kids, I enrolled in a Ph.D. program in philosophy. I devoted myself to smoking endless rounds of cigarettes while debating the finer points of existentialism.

To my parents' horror, I enjoyed shopping in an Army and Navy Salvage store, selecting a gas-mask bag as a purse and stashing lipsticks in the slots slated for bullets. I laughed at the normalcy of Tupperware parties, wedding showers, church suppers, and all the everyday things that ordinary folks embraced.

Then one summer, my perspective changed. My boyfriend and I were headed to San Francisco for a summer vacation and took a short detour into Mexico. On the way back, the border patrol took one look at the battered VW and pulled us over for inspection. As we stood by, quaking in fear, an officer unearthed a tiny candy tin, containing just enough of an illegal herb to land us in jail.

As I wept on a bony cot in a lonely cell that night, normal life started assuming a new luster. Even though I was a self-proclaimed atheist at the time, I found myself begging God for help. He must have heard me because a minor miracle happened the next morning. When my boyfriend and I appeared in court, the kindly old judge surveyed our swollen eyes and clean records, and set us free. We nixed the vacation idea and scurried back home to get jobs.

My days of living on the edge were over. I never shoplifted again and I became scrupulous about obeying traffic laws. Eventually, I married a nice man and landed a regular job. Today I carry a sensible purse, which is roomy enough to stash treats for my goddaughter, and I appreciate a decent piece of Tupperware.

In the liturgical year, the special seasons of Advent, Christmas, Lent and Easter are preceded by long stretches of what is called Ordinary Time. Although I used to scorn Ordinary Time because it lacked the shine of Christmas and the exuberance of Easter, now I love it. When I read newspaper stories about the demons that come out of nowhere to sink their fangs into the hearts of everyday folks, bringing car wrecks, illnesses, and wars, I can see the advantage of a boring life.

If my younger self could see me now, she'd run shrieking away. I go to bed early, eat regular meals, plus the recommended daily allowance of chocolate, and do crossword puzzles. And in bed each night, I thank God for another ordinary day. The "same old, same old" really can be a blessing in disguise.

Sacred Heart—June 18

Within Thy Wounds

IN the newspaper photo, the women are wearing brightly colored scarves, while the men are dressed drably and hunched over. The caption tells the story: The family is escaping from their home before the bombs start falling. The faces, so sad and weary, are achingly familiar. The eyes look into the camera with a sense of resignation that I have seen in the expressions of other people fleeing desperate situations. The war will crush everyday people like these; a river of blood will be spilled.

Blood makes me think of the name some people use to describe someone who opposes war: "bleeding heart liberal." And then I remember the many paintings that show Jesus pointing to his heart, exposed in his chest. In some paintings, his sacred heart is framed in flames; in others, it is pierced by thorns.

My own heart breaks for the families that were not able to flee the terror. I also weep for the soldiers, on both sides, who have died—and for their grieving families. War is ugly, brutal and bloody. And the lesson that violence only breeds more violence comes straight from Jesus in the Garden of Gethsemane.

When the angry crowd led by Judas arrives with swords and clubs, the soldiers grab Jesus to arrest him, and a friend rushes to his defense. He draws a sword and attacks the high priest's servant, cutting off his ear. Many would say the friend's action was justified because the friend was trying to protect an innocent man. But that's not how Jesus sees it. "Stop, no more of this!" he protests, and tells the friend to put away the weapon because "All who take the sword will perish by the sword." Jesus then heals the servant, which is a remarkable act and a great lesson to us: The last miracle before his death is ministering to an enemy.

Taking the sword can stand for violence of any kind. Bombing, shooting, burning, pillaging, maiming–the whole ghastly roll call of war–are antithetical to Christ's radical message of love. On the cross, he forgave the men who had beaten and mocked him, spit on him, and pierced his hands and feet. He came long ago to instill a revolutionary lesson about love, and all these years later, it is still so hard to get it right.

Years ago, Mahatma Gandhi, a devout proponent of nonviolent resistance to evil, suggested that he would convert to Christianity if he ever met a Christian who lived according to Christ's teachings. I have to say that if Gandhi had met me, I don't think he would have rushed to the baptismal font. Truth to tell, I have plenty of dark and brooding thoughts in my heart. I sometimes ignore my kind impulses and hurt people instead.

The brooding eyes of that family in the newspaper photo haunt me in my dreams. Maybe it's because their faces are so darn familiar. They look like my own aunts, uncles, nieces and nephews. They look so much like me. And today, as I sit in the comfort of my living room, gazing at the tiny blossoms on the trees, I am lamenting that, across the globe, lives are crumbling, children are screaming, fires are blazing and people are dying. And I can almost hear the words of the one whose heart still bleeds for peace: "Stop, no more of this!"

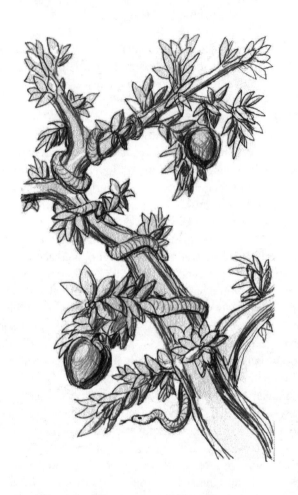

Father's Day
Third Sunday in June

My Rock

THE popular "whatever" mentality worries me. Do you want sweet tea or lemonade? Whatever. Fried fish or chicken? Whatever. The "anything goes" that lurks at the heart of this mindset is especially scary when applied to life's big issues. Shall we go to this church or that? Get involved in the soup kitchen or not? Whatever.

Remember when you were a child and went to your dad for help with a broken toy? Dad didn't shrug and say, "Whatever." He got out the old tool kit and went to work. As a teen, maybe you asked him for advice when your heart was broken. He pondered your problem seriously and probably gave you the same advice his dear old dad had given him.

Maybe his advice seemed a trifle out of date since he was, after all, rummaging around in the wisdom of generations past to uncover a jewel or two. Still, you could count on Dad to stick by absolute standards. He knew God wasn't kidding when He handed out the Ten Commandments. Dad knew they weren't a rough draft.

My own dad gave me a glimpse of what God must be like. He faced the rather onerous task of doling out punishment in the days when "Wait until your father gets home" was a common expression. Often, his idea of discipline meant sternly removing his belt and chasing my sister and me around the house, but rarely catching us. Still, we kicked up quite a fuss because we were afraid of him. And later he must have felt contrite because he bought us comic books as a sign of mercy.

When I learned about God the Father, it made sense that He had not created an "anything goes" world but instead gave unbending instructions to our first parents in Eden. And when they disobeyed Him, He doled out real punishments. Problem is, today's "whatever" crowd apparently believes there are no consequences for bad actions or wrong choices. Are you having premarital sex or dabbling in drugs? Cheating on your taxes? Or on your spouse? *"Whatever,"* whispers the little voice in your head. The same one that assures you, *"Everyone else is doing it."*

The anything-goes mentality suggests everyone's opinion is equally valuable. This means I can worship a six-headed beast with a tail and you can worship the Judeo-Christian God Who created the universe in seven days—and we'd both be right. Taken to its logical, politically correct conclusion, this radically permissive attitude suggests there can't be a Hell because everyone is just bumbling along doing the best they can.

Still, as any good dad can attest, "anything goes" is the recipe for disaster. Fathering means setting standards and sticking with them. It means knowing the difference between good and evil. A father who truly loves his child does not cave in to the whims of a changing world; instead, he knows he must sometimes say, "No."

When we pray to our heavenly Father, He doesn't always give us what we want, but He always sends us what is ultimately good for us. And when we are in the depths of despair, crying and needy, we can turn to our Father and be confident that He will hear our cry. And know that He will never reply, "Whatever."

Midsummer Night's Eve
June 21

Light from Light

I'VE always wondered what the Garden of Eden was like before the Fall. Genesis tells us God walked around in the cool of the morning and talked with Adam and Eve. There was an abundance of trees, and all manner of creeping and flying things. And on midsummer night's eve, when our yard seems overrun by flora and fauna, I find my memories running to the taste of Eden I had as a child.

Growing up in Miami, I started counting the days until summer some time in March. Although I was an A student at school, I hated the endless grind of multiplication tables and spelling bees, and the feeling of imminent doom when the teacher called out my name. Summer meant I was free, I could sleep late, go to the library and come home with a stack of books that didn't need the teacher's seal of approval. We had a pool nearby, and my sister and I spent hours floating around and pretending we were turtles.

When we wearied of that, we could turn on the lawn sprinklers and race around making believe we were horses. The distant jingle of the ice cream truck made us go berserk, trying to scrounge up change before chasing the truck down the street. On blistering hot summer days, I made the luscious discovery that fudge Popsicles make a very decent lunch.

Our modest turquoise house, located at 6090 S.W. 12th Street, was surrounded by all manner of growing, creeping and flying things. We had coconut palms, plus mango, banana, Key lime, grapefruit and orange trees. Gaudy red hibiscus, lusciously sweet gardenias and lizards that somehow could change colors while you watched them were our everyday miracles. Mornings we had bird choirs belting out prayers, with frogs, cicadas and katydids taking up the slack at night.

Summer meant my sister and I could retire our starchy school uniforms and don shorts and flip-flops. Better yet, we could ignore our dad's dire warnings about snakes hiding in the grass, and traipse around barefoot. Somedays, we just lived in our bathing suits. It was heaven on earth, but like most earthly paradises, ours had a few wrinkles. My mom was a teacher and once school was out, she had a list of household projects a yard long. There were jalousie windows to wash, screens to (groan) scrub and closets to clean out. Unless Rosemary and I figured out a way to evade the ominous sound of mop and broom as our mom approached our bedroom, we were cornered.

Still, we loved summer. Once we'd done our chores, we could grab a stack of comics and walk to the pool or play Monopoly to our heart's content. To this day, the taste of an Almond Joy bar, the scent of coconut suntan lotion and the distant giggling of children in a swimming pool make my heart turn over with a longing for those Miami summers.

Somehow I thought I'd always live with my parents and sister in that little turquoise house. It never occurred to me, when I said my prayers, to thank God for all the everyday things that made life so sweet. And I can't help but wonder if Adam and Eve's original sin stemmed from a lack of gratitude. Maybe, if they had realized the blessings of their glorious garden, they would have bypassed the forbidden fruit. And who knows? Maybe they could have been happy and free in Paradise forever. Just like children, eating Popsicles and prancing through the sprinklers on a summer day in Miami.

St. Mary Magdalene
July 22

Vale of Tears

So many scenes from Scripture would translate beautifully to the big screen. There is the terrified Peter grasping Jesus' hand while the storm rages at sea. Lazarus, emerging dumbfounded and dazed from the tomb. And the tragic kiss of Judas.

My favorite scene features a woman washing a man's feet with her tears. The man is Jesus, and he is dining at a Pharisee's home, when suddenly a weeping woman makes her way into the room. She kneels before Jesus, then uses her tears to cleanse the dust from his feet. Talk about a moment of high drama. And talk about a mystery: I've often wondered how many tears it would take to wash a man's feet.

The woman isn't named in the scene, and although there's been much debate over her identity, tradition suggests she was Mary Magdalene. Tradition also pictures Mary as one of those bad girls that respectable folks avoid. Today she might sport stiletto heels, a skin-tight dress and generous cleavage. The woman's reputation evidently precedes her, because the host wants her to leave, until Jesus defends her. And the words he utters could become the slogan for all the bad girls in the world: "Her many sins have been forgiven for she loved much."

I can relate to Mary Magdalene. I was raised on the straight and narrow path, with all the usual warnings from my mom about men. As soon as I got to college, though, I started falling in with the wrong crowd. It seems I had a penchant for attracting Mr. Wrong. If a man were a brooding, handsome guy with a reputation as a Romeo, invariably I would fall for him. I assured myself he would change his ways and we'd have a relationship like you see in fairy tales, where everyone lives happily ever after. Unfortunately, happy endings kept evading me and before long, I was on to the next guy.

My generation was spoon-fed the belief that behavioral differences between men and women weren't biologically based but resulted instead from upbringing. Women were encouraged to level the playing field by imitating men. This logic led to an inevitable, scary conclusion: If men could jump into bed with women they hardly knew and suffer little emotional harm, then women should follow suit. Before long, sex became a recreational sport, and "free love" became our mantra.

I soon discovered, however, that hard-wired emotional differences surely exist between the genders. My male friends seemed unscathed by dabbling in casual sex, while my girlfriends and I spent hours crying on each other's shoulders, confiding about the awful ways men were treating us. We thought we were modern women, but our hearts were stubbornly old-fashioned. Deep inside, we wanted the same thing our moms and grandmothers had longed for: We wanted to be loved and cherished, not used.

Maybe that's why Mary Magdalene was weeping, when she knelt before Jesus. Maybe she was remembering all the different beds, and all the men who had betrayed her.

After the crucifixion, we see Mary crying again, and her tears draw Jesus back from the dead. "Woman, why are you weeping?" he asks, as she stands at the tomb. He knew the answer, of course. She was grieving because she thought she'd lost the man who cherished her without conditions and labels.

Mary Magdalene remains a symbol of hope for all the women who feel dragged down and broken. For all the women who've strayed from the path, whether their detour was alcoholism, drugs, promiscuity or prostitution. She stands for God's mercy and love for all the world's bad girls. How wonderful that we get another chance, and another, and another.

Transfiguration—August 6

Dappled Things

MY husband and I are standing on the dock, marveling as a dolphin dances through the serene waters of the Gulf of Mexico. Nearby, two local fishermen are drinking coffee and rehashing the events of a party from the night before. The big mammal flaps his tail vigorously against the water, while his powerful exhalations explode in the stillness. Meanwhile, the men, taking slow sips from their mugs, seem lost in a world of memories. By the time they glance at the water, the dolphin is long gone.

I understand, though. When we're vacationing at the seashore it's easy to be fully awake to every moment. Our eyes relish the sight of gaudy tropical blooms and clouds as plump as homemade biscuits. At home, though, we sometimes take the local wonders for granted.

Strolling down the road near home one evening, I was lost in thought. Wondering if I had enough flour to make brownies that night, I almost missed the show unfolding before my eyes. There were mockingbirds crooning a medley of tunes, a gardenia bush bristling with fancy blooms and a baby beaming me a toothless grin. I was so caught up in my own ruminations that I was in danger of overlooking these small delights. Just like the fishermen missed the dolphin.

A few weeks ago, a man new to our neighborhood stopped by our house to ask directions. While the adults studied a map, the man's tiny son crouched in the driveway and stared at the ground. During a pause in our conversation, we realized the baby was studying an ant that was creeping along the path. "He's like that," the father said. "He can spend hours just looking at things."

That baby was a great teacher for me. He showed me that God packages little gifts in each moment of an ordinary day, but we often fail to pay attention. Most days I walk fuzzy brained to my office, unaware of the miracles of a newborn morning. When I remind myself to pay attention, I'll look up and see a leftover sliver of moon decorating the sky and red-tailed hawks swimming through the clouds.

On an ordinary day long ago, Jesus climbed a mountain with his friends, who suddenly saw him transfigured, ablaze with divine light, and talking with Elijah and Moses. It would be easy to conclude that you must do something exotic like climbing a mountain to encounter the divine, but the truth is that God hides in the heart of every person. As Gandhi said, "If you don't see God in the next person you meet, there is no need to look further."

The recipe for meeting God isn't that tricky, but it takes effort. Like a baby studying an ant, you have to give each person in life your full attention. You can't be juggling the cell phone and the to-do list while your husband tells you about his day. You can't be reading the paper and eating your cereal while a toddler chats about last night's dreams. After all, if Jesus' friends had been lost in a fog of memories about a fishing trip, they might have missed that wonder on the mountain.

The world is abloom in miracles. We can stand on the dock and enjoy the dance of the dolphins; watch an ant moseying down a path. We can behold the light in the eyes of our sweetheart when he turns to us and says, "I love you." We needn't take a vacation to encounter God. We can find Him in our own backyard, if we just look.

Labor Day
First Monday in September

World Without End

MY watch broke last week, and my first impulse was to hunt down a repairman. But then I wondered what life would be like if I were freed, for just a while, from the tyranny of time.

Why is it that when we are children Saturday stretches out like a vast continent that we march across, squeezing ounces of sweet juice from each passing second? As adults, we mourn time's passing in the busyness of everyday life. We seem entrenched in our endless tasks that leave us feeling that the day has slipped by without our noticing it.

Labor Day weekend gives us a chance for a last summer vacation. Not surprisingly, the word "vacation" shares something in common with "vacant" and rightly so, because on getaways we empty the usual concerns from our hearts. And how rich and full time seems when the lawn isn't shooting you accusing glances and the furniture isn't begging in a piteous voice to be dusted.

My birthday falls at the end of summer vacation season, right before Labor Day. I must confess that, with each passing year, I am so grateful my husband doesn't alert the fire department before igniting the candles on my cake. "Make a wish," he suggests, and I wish I could have some of the years back. Let's face it: Time still has me in its clutches, even if I'm not wearing my watch. Whenever I turn on my computer, walk into the kitchen or get into my car, time rears its head, reminding me of the unfinished business of ordinary life. There are floors to sweep, laundry to fold, groceries to buy and weeds to pull. "Leave me alone," I want to scream at the smug face of the clock. "I'll never get it all done, even in a 48-hour day."

When you are constantly on the go, always plugged in to computer, cell phone or TV, and trying to do two things at once, your relationship with God can seem like one more chore on the to-do list. Have I said my prayers, attended church, tithed and volunteered? Yes, but I am still so frazzled that God seems far away.

The prophet Elijah scurried around looking for God, but couldn't find Him in the spectacle of an earthquake, the dazzle of fire or the dramatic rush of wind. Then he hid his face in his cloak and discovered God in a tiny whispering sound. That story reveals a way to slow down time, but it is not easy. You must put aside your books, turn off the TV and phone, relinquish snacks and other diversions, sit down in a quiet spot and do nothing for a while.

Thomas Merton in *The Inner Experience* suggests we all have two selves. The chatty, busy, fearful self is the personality that is always rushing from home to job to store. The inner self he describes as the breath of the divine. To hear the shy voice of that inner self, we have to do what is really tough. We have to pause from our frantic schedules, sit in a chair and surrender our crowded hearts to God.

Only when we take a respite from the busyness of everyday life can we unveil the deep hidden self that never glances at the watch. It doesn't need to, because it owns eternity.

Exaltation of the Holy Cross
September 14

Anima Christi

WHAT can I possibly say to a friend whose baby died before ever being born? This was the question I asked myself as I sat at my desk, reading the heart-rending e-mail message.

My friend had begun the lovely task of planning names and gathering tiny garments. And then on a recent doctor's visit, came the awful news: There was no longer a heartbeat within her womb.

What do I say to a neighbor who has been stricken with cancer? A devoted father and a man of deep faith, he faces a grueling regimen of chemotherapy.

"God often writes straight with crooked lines" is a Portuguese proverb that helps when things are looking bleak. And so often, when our friends are in trouble, our first response is trying to fix the crooked lines. This was my reaction, as I found myself searching for a book about emotional healing after a miscarriage to give my friend. Until I realized that no book could mend a shattered heart.

"Let me know what I can do to help" are words that so easily spring from our lips when our friends are struggling with catastrophes. Problem is, a person whose world has just come crashing down may not know what he needs. It becomes a huge task just to get dressed, have breakfast and go through the motions of everyday life.

I sent flowers and a sympathy card to the friends who lost their baby. I left baked goodies and cards in the mailbox for my neighbor and his family. Still, there is the dilemma of what to say to folks whose world has turned topsy-turvy. Especially when a family member dies, we tend to avoid the widow or the bereaved children because we're afraid of saying something stupid or wrong.

Recently I attended a talk by Father John Murphy at our church, and he pointed out that the worst thing to say to people in great distress is "You'll get over it." He was right, of course, for if someone had assured me years ago that I would "get over" my dear mother's death, the words would have cut me to the quick.

St. Thomas More, a martyr, wrote a prayer that goes, "The things that we pray for, dear Lord, give us the grace to labor for." His prayer reminds us that God's work gets done through us. We are the hands of God in the everyday world. He is the one who prompts us to send a card and pick up the phone.

Mother Teresa had many volunteers who gave her nuns a hand with the day-to-day chores in her homes for the sick and dying. She knew, however, that many people who wanted to help were unable to, since they were bedridden or disabled. She entrusted to these folks a simple, yet life-changing activity. She asked them to pray for the suffering people of the world, which was work they could do from bed or wheelchair.

When our friends are struggling to decipher the crooked lines of their lives, we can visit them to assure them of our love. We can bake a cake, drop off a casserole or baby-sit the kids.

Still, I've come to realize there is no best thing to say to a friend whose baby never was born. Or to a neighbor diagnosed with cancer. All we can do is pray with the certainty that God will send them the words they need to hear.

St. Thérèse of the Child Jesus
October 1

Least of These

I'M hunkered down on the couch, holding the yarn with my left hand and the crochet hook in my right. I'm supposed to wrap the yarn around the hook and then poke it through the . . . Oh, heck! I've dropped a stitch, for what seems like the thousandth time.

It's little wonder, though, because I've always been hopeless at the feminine arts. In home economics class, I watched in awe as other girls turned out darling dresses with matching purses. Meanwhile, I dragged home voluminous garments that resembled laundry bags. In 4-H club, the boys learned about livestock and crops, while the girls hemmed delicate dishtowels. You could tell which towels were mine a mile away: They were the crooked ones embroidered with bloodstains.

Undaunted, I tackled the womanly art of table setting. Forks here, knives there, and glasses on the right—or was it the left? Too bad no one believed me when I protested that the forks and spoons switched places when my back was turned.

Every fall, I neglect these lessons of childhood and start dreaming of the gifts I will make for Christmas. This year, lady friends at work are crocheting up a storm, and I figured I would climb on board. After all, how hard could it be to turn out a nice afghan? I usually write in the afternoons, but recently I've been plopping down on the couch with my yarn instead. Huge chunks of time melt away as I struggle to decipher the instructions, which read: "DC three times and then YO. Repeat six times." Huh?

Friends are producing glowing scarves in all colors of the rainbow, but all I have to show for my efforts so far is a tear-stained instruction sheet and a snarl of yarn that looks like spaghetti on amphetamines. Why, oh why, I lament, did God give me such clumsy hands?

After sniveling a bit, I took some comfort in realizing that St. Thérèse of the Child Jesus wrestled with a similar dilemma. In her diary, *Story of a Soul,* Thérèse wondered why God seemed to lavish some people with graces, while being apparently skimpy with others. This simple girl, who became known as the Little Flower, found her answer by observing nature. Every flower couldn't have the extravagant beauty of a rose, she noted. And she reminded herself that God loves even simple flowers like violets and daisies. "Perfection consists in . . . being what He wills us to be," she wrote.

Sometimes we forget we all have talents that are gifts from God. The abilities to garden, sing, cook, repair things and do carpentry are all signs of His generosity. I greatly admire women whose gift is managing herds of little children. I have marveled to see Romana, a teacher at our church school, walking serenely along as a line of children placidly trail her. If you asked me to keep order among third-graders, even for an hour, I might suffer a serious meltdown.

Sometimes we take our God-given talents for granted. "Oh, that's nothing," we say as friends marvel at our tender piecrust or thriving garden. As for me, I suppose I often take writing for granted too. "Oh, that's nothing," I'll say when someone admires an essay, even though I may have spent hours sprucing up the nouns and tweaking the verbs.

Taking my cue form St. Thérèse, I have stashed away the yarn and returned to writing in the afternoons. I admit there are still times when I long to be a splendid rose when it comes to the feminine arts. But I am learning to accept my status as a humble daisy.

Feast of Guardian Angels
October 2

Gratia Plena

I WALK into the hospital with a sense of dread. I've fasted from midnight for the upcoming surgery this afternoon, and I'm fighting a coffee-withdrawal headache along with a bad case of nerves.

My doctor suggested the surgery as part of a routine checkup, but as anyone who has weathered a cancer diagnosis will attest, the possibility of recurrence perches on your shoulder like a scowling devil. Nothing in the medical world seems routine anymore.

Last night, I prayed fervently for God to chase that bleak devil away. "Dear Lord, give me the grace I need to get through the day. Send me an angel to protect me."

Soon, a little plump nurse calls me into a back room. She gives me a hospital gown, a cap and a pair of booties, with instructions to undress and put my clothes in a big plastic bag.

When she leaves, I contemplate escaping out the back door, but I know this is a childish impulse, so instead I don the blue gown, open the door and hand the nurse the bag containing my clothes.

She beckons to a nearby hospital bed and I obediently climb in. Glancing around the room, I observe the predictable framed prints of sad flowers amid all the syringes, thermometers and other contraptions that adorn a hospital room. "Where are you, God?" I wonder, as my tears start to flow. "You seem so far away."

The little nurse notices my distress and comes over to cover me with a blanket. "Now, there's nothing to cry about," she says as sweetly as if she were speaking to a child. "You just pray and set your mind at ease. Everything will be fine."

Her words help stem the tide of tears, until I realize that she is about to hook me up to the IV. Remembering the last surgery, I brace myself for the needle's sharp stab of pain. But just then, a tall, brightly made-up woman in a nurse's outfit appears at the side of the bed.

She takes my other hand in hers and leans down to beam me a big smile.

"Hi, Lorraine," she smiles, "I'm going to be with you today in the operating room." Then she pauses a moment before delivering the punch line: "My name is Grace."

My mother and grandmother were named Grace, I tell her. "And it's my middle name," I babble in excitement. "I think this is a good sign."

As we are chuckling over the coincidence, the other nurse slides the needle into my hand, but all I feel is a light touch, as gentle as a butterfly's wing. Moments later, in the operating room, I ask Grace for a favor. "Will you pray the Our Father with me?" I whisper groggily, as the anesthesia begins coursing through my veins. She takes my hand in hers and looks tenderly into my eyes. We get all the way to "amen" before I black out.

That night, snuggled down in my own bed at last, I thank God for the surgeon's good report—and for sending me an angel named Grace. As I drift off to sleep, I recall the saying about God working in mysterious ways. And I wonder if part of the mystery is that He enjoys playing a trick on us every now and again. Just to see us smile.

St. Francis of Assisi
October 4

Bright Wings

M Y husband and I are taking a fall getaway on Cedar Key, Florida. As we are unpacking our bags in our rented condo, I swing open the porch doors and scan the shore. I'm hoping for a glimpse of the white duck.

This tiny island boasts fancy birds like osprey, roseate spoonbills and wood ducks, but there is only one white duck. And on our many visits, the sounds of her contented quacking have become as dear to me as the whispers of the surf. Over the years, my husband and I have kept a journal of the wildlife we've spotted, with typical entries reading: "Saw dolphins and otters today, and of course, the white duck."

I loved watching the white duck frolicking among the colorful wood ducks because she seemed oblivious to the fact that she was different. Recalling my stint as a pudgy child who never quite fit in with other kids, I admired her devil-may-care attitude. Today, though, there is no sign of my feathered friend, and this makes me nervous, especially when I recall that we saw a fox running loose on our last visit.

Later, Patty, who works in the condo office, confirms my worst fears. Seems she had discovered the poor duck huddled beneath a car, badly shaken and bloodied, and called Ed, who runs a wildlife rescue team. He whisked away the bird to the veterinary college at the University of Florida, but two weeks later, the poor girl died. We both have tears in our eyes as Patty tells me the story, but I remind myself that the duck lived a good life, paddling through the surf and enjoying handouts from the tourists. I also have a very strong feeling that the white duck is in heaven. It may seem shocking to some folks to postulate that a duck could get into heaven, but I sometimes feel that the birds and the beasts might have less trouble getting through the Pearly Gates than some humans. Animals don't build weapons of mass destruction, and they don't research ways to wipe out other species with chemical agents. Animals don't spew pollution into the air or destroy forests to build malls.

Of course, there is plenty of blood shed in the world of nature, but the animal that attacked the duck was just following its instincts. Animals don't have consciences like human beings do, and they are certainly incapable of sinning. We humans, on the other hand, know it is wrong to plot revenge and to be greedy and cruel, but we do these things anyway. Fortunately, humans also perform stunning acts of compassion, as shown by the firefighters who gave their lives at the World Trade Center after the terrorist attacks on September 11, 2001, as well as the many volunteers who routinely put in long hours at shelters and hospitals.

Jesus said the key to entering the kingdom of heaven was becoming like a little child. And I sometimes wonder if animals perk up our spirits so much because they are as spontaneous and innocent as children. Surely the Creator must have a special place in His big heart for His furred and feathered beasts. After all, the Bible reminds us that after God made wild animals and birds, He was quite pleased.

Perhaps God will be big hearted enough to look the other way some day and let a sinner like me sneak into heaven. And if He does, I can imagine myself making a mental note: "Saw the angels and the saints, the choir of heavenly hosts, and, of course, the white duck."

Halloween—October 31

Seen and Unseen

A FRIEND confided that her little boy plans to be a zebra for Halloween, or as he put it: "black and white neigh-neigh." The little guy already knows it can be great fun to don a mask now and again, and Halloween presents a fine opportunity.

As Halloween approaches, I've been reflecting on the many disguises I've worn over the years. I started out as a plump baby, shown in photos gazing rather morosely through the bars of my playpen. According to family legend, neighbors would exclaim, "What a cute little girl!" and I would startle them by uttering a word my big sister, Rosemary, had taught me. "Dope!"

One of my first roles in life was that of copycat. No matter what Rosemary said or did, I mimicked her. If she ordered chocolate pie at the restaurant, so did I, and if she wanted a new teddy bear, I was there too. Before long, I had gained a nickname from my Uncle Savy that trailed me into adulthood: "Me Too."

Later photos show a dutiful Catholic schoolgirl, attired in crisp, carefully ironed uniforms and spotless saddle oxfords. This girl said her rosary, attended Mass, lit votive candles and brought home report cards studded with gold stars. Unfortunately, things got really scary when I was 17 and left home for the University of Florida. Embracing atheism with a vengeance, I was eager to trade rosary beads and crucifixes for love beads and miniskirts. Before long, I assumed the disguise of a full-fledged hippie. Photos show me wearing a peace symbol around my neck and a dress so abbreviated that today it would serve as a blouse.

When God did eventually draw me back to Him, He didn't use the standard arguments I knew by heart from philosophy texts, but rather the everyday details of the heart. Many years after college, after I had married, my husband returned from a business trip to announce that he had "out of the blue" stopped at St. Patrick's Cathedral. He had decided to light votive candles for his father and my parents, who were deceased. My first thought was: "Oh, no, I never prayed for the repose of Mommy's and Daddy's souls!"

Shortly after, I started reading a book that had sat untouched on my shelves for years. It was *Seven Storey Mountain,* Thomas Merton's stirring tale of his own conversion, and I suspected it had not fallen into my hands by chance. Little by little, the mask of atheism fell away, and I soon found myself on my knees in a Catholic church with a simple request: "Help me to believe." That prayer was answered, and eventually I returned to the Church, and my husband converted to Catholicism.

Sometimes I despair over the masks I wore in my younger life. I drank too much, partied too heartily, and, yes, when that huge, hand-made cigarette was passed to me, I did inhale. Sometimes I cringe over the younger versions of me, groaning over the stupid and immoral things I did.

Then I remember that in God's eyes, a thousand years pass as a second. Perhaps, when He looks at us, He sees at a glance all the costumes we have worn, starting with the moment when He first gave us life in the womb. He sees us in the playpen and dressed as a zebra at Halloween. He sees the wild days of our youth and the more placid days of middle age.

And no matter how cleverly we try to disguise ourselves, He loves us nonetheless. Because He knows that, deep down inside, we are always His children.

All Souls Day—November 2

Sweet Sacraments

I AM in the kitchen, whipping up a fig cake from Big Mama's recipe, written in her own hand. And as I sift the flour and grate the nutmeg, I remember my husband's two grandmothers and how dearly I loved them.

About 10 years ago, my husband, his sister, Lisa, and I traveled to Brandon, Mississippi, to visit their father's mom, Sadie Murray, who was known to the family as Big Mama. I knew that Big Mama had been the wife of a sharecropper and had raised seven children. I also had learned from family stories that she was known for her love of fishing, baking and making afghans for her grandchildren. All in all, she sounded like a down-home Southern grandma. And frankly I was a little nervous about meeting her.

As we approached the door of her simple little apartment, I wondered if she had cherished a hope that her grandson would marry a blue-eyed Southern belle. I hoped she wouldn't be disappointed that he had instead chosen an olive-skinned Italian-American girl with traces of Yankee in her speech. We knocked on the door and suddenly there she was, a plump lady in a flowery housedress, who wrapped her two grown grandchildren in her arms. A moment later, she dispelled my fears by giving me a huge hug too—and declaring me pretty.

That night, she treated the whole slew of aunts, uncles and grandchildren to an "all-you-can-eat" fried catfish meal at Cindy's Restaurant and then back to her apartment for slabs of her homemade fig cake. As I devoured a second helping, she insisted that I call her Big Mama, like the rest of the family, and in that moment I felt right at home.

My husband's maternal grandmother was very different from Big Mama. She was a slim lady whose children and grandchildren called her Gladys. She liked reading *National Geographic,* traveling to Greece and tooling down the country roads of Rome, Georgia, in her Mercedes.

Gladys Lester lived with Callie, a small black dog with a reputation for taking nips out of strangers. Which suited Gladys just fine, since she lived alone. Upon first meeting Callie, I caught a glimpse of bared teeth and cringed, expecting her to lunge. Instead, Callie surprised me by planting a wet smooch on my hand, while Gladys proclaimed: "She knows you're family."

The two grandmothers took to mailing me recipes with short notes attached. Big Mama sent me the fig cake recipe and invited us to go fishing with her. Gladys sent her recipe for lemon pudding, adding that her children, Lou and Russell, had been known to devour the entire dessert in one sitting. In one note, she mentioned that Callie was outside the kitchen, snoozing in a patch of sun in the yard.

Whenever I make the fig cake, I remember Big Mama's hug and regret that we never returned to go fishing with her. And whenever I serve the lemon pudding, I imagine Gladys in her Mercedes and the little dog grinning in the sun.

Big Mama is gone now, as are Gladys and Callie, but every Sunday, I feel close to the trio when I pray for them after Holy Communion, the sacred meal served at the altar.

I also feel their presence in my kitchen while I'm cooking. And sometimes I envision the two grandmothers sitting on a porch in heaven, trading recipes. I also see Callie resting nearby, begging for crumbs and pining for a stranger to show up, so she might take a little nip.

Thanksgiving
Fourth Thursday in November

Chipmunk Moments

MY goddaughter is here to have lunch and bake cookies with me while her mom has cafeteria duty at her brother's school. As we are unpacking her lunch bag, we unearth a paper napkin with a cheery heart pattern.

"Oh, look at the hearts!" I exclaim—and the child doesn't miss a beat. "That's because Mommy loves me," she explains.

Once lunch is over, we head to the kitchen to make a batch of chocolate chip cookies. But first Sarah grabs a wooden spoon and parades around, swinging it like a baton. Once she tires of that, we get down to the serious business of measuring and sifting. And when I notice out of the corner of my eye that the child can't resist popping a few chocolate chips into her mouth, I marvel at the love I also feel for her.

Sarah makes me laugh on the dreariest days by wearing my eyeglasses and exclaiming, "I'm Aunt Awaine," or pointing at the baby in the arms of the statue of Mother Mary and announcing with a gigantic grin, "That's Baby JEE-sus!"

I love her most of all because she reminds me that we are all infinitely precious in the eyes of God. With billions of people on the planet today and so many who lived here before us, it is hard sometimes to realize that God cherishes each of us. Still, we can say with the prophet Jeremiah, "Lord, before I existed, you beheld me and called me by name."

God calls our names every day, although He sometimes chooses messengers that are somewhat mysterious, like a bird belting out songs in our yard or fragile flowers shyly raising their heads in the garden. In my life, chipmunks have been the messengers of divine grace.

I've been a big fan of these little creatures ever since childhood days when I would visit my Aunt Maddy and Uncle

August and start the day standing beneath a tree with a handful of nuts, calling to the friendly chipmunk that lived there. As I trembled with joy, Chippy would scurry down, grab a nut from my hand, stuff it into his cheek and scoot back to safety.

Ever since then, whenever one of these elusive creatures dances across my path, I see the moment as a special gift from God. And the ordinary events that remind me of the Creator's love, I call my chipmunk moments.

My mind returns to the present moment as I notice that little Sarah is creating a big snowdrift of four on the floor. I don't reprimand her though, because she will learn neatness later, and for now we are having too much fun. Once the cookies are baked, her mom comes to pick her up– and we sit around munching on cookies and complimenting the child on her baking skills. "Aunt Awaine helped," Sarah notes, reaching for seconds.

Then just as she and her mom are heading out the door, it happens. This beloved girl, her face smudged with chocolate, runs over, smooches me on the arm, and scoots away. It is just a tiny gesture and quickly over, but later, as I sweep the flour from the floor, I turn the memory over in my mind like a jewel. And I thank God for another chipmunk moment.

ABOUT THE AUTHOR

Lorraine V. Murray (originally Viscardi) is the author of two previous books: *Grace Notes* (Catholic Book Publishing/Resurrection Press) and *Why Me? Why Now? Finding Hope When You Have Breast Cancer* (Ave Maria Press). She writes a column called "Grace Notes" for the Faith and Values section of *The Atlanta Journal-Constitution,* and is a regular contributor to *The Georgia Bulletin,* the newspaper of the Catholic Archdiocese of Atlanta. Her work also appears in the magazine *America.*

Lorraine grew up in Miami, graduated from Immaculata-La Salle High School and received a master's degree in English and a doctorate in philosophy from the University of Florida. A former college instructor, Lorraine now works mornings in the Pitts Theology Library at Emory University. In her spare time, she likes to bake and read British mysteries.

Lorraine lives in Decatur, Georgia, with her husband, Jef, an artist who created the sketches for this book. Their pets include Scruffy and Wuffy the gerbils, Tinker Bell the cat, and an elusive hamster named Ignatius.

Jef's artwork can be seen on www.jefmurray.com. To contact Lorraine, write: lorrainevmurray@yahoo.com.

OTHER BOOKS OF INTEREST

www.catholicbookpublishing.com

Additional Titles Published by Resurrection Press, a Catholic Book Publishing Imprint

For a free catalog call 1-800-892-6657
www.catholicbookpublishing.com